Ancient China

John Hinton

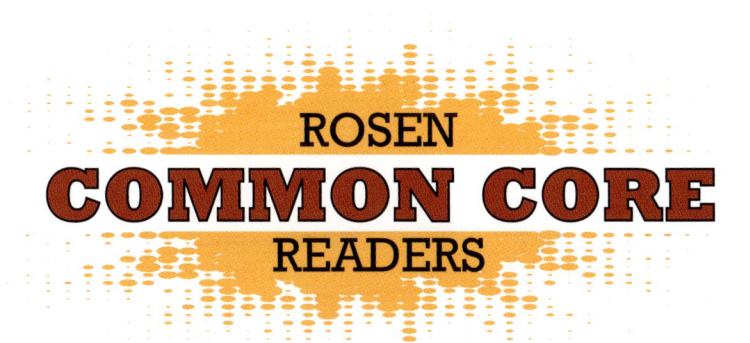

ROSEN
COMMON CORE
READERS

Rosen Classroom

New York

Published in 2014 by The Rosen Publishing Group, Inc.
29 East 21st Street, New York, NY 10010

Copyright © 2014 by The Rosen Publishing Group, Inc.

All rights reserved. No part of this book may be reproduced in any form without permission in writing from the publisher, except by a reviewer.

Book Design: Jon D'Rozario

Photo Credits: Cover zhu difeng/Shutterstock.com; pp. 3, 4, 6, 8, 10, 12, 14, 16, 18, 20, 22, 23, 24 (background) Irina_QQQ/Shutterstock.com; p. 5 (river) cnyy/Shutterstock.com; p. 5 (map) Olinchuk/Shutterstock.com; p. 7 DEA/G. DAGLI ORTI/Getty Images; p. 9 Jun Mu/Shutterstock.com; p. 11 toonman/Shutterstock.com; p. 13 British Library/Robana/Hulton Fine Art Collection/Getty Images; p. 15 IMAGEMORE Co, Ltd./IMAGEMORE Co, Ltd./Getty Images; p. 17 fotohunter/Shutterstock.com; p. 19 Philip Lange/Shutterstock.com; pp. 21, 22 Hung Chung Chih/Shutterstock.com.

ISBN: 978-1-4777-2483-5
6-pack ISBN: 978-1-4777-2484-2

Manufactured in the United States of America

CPSIA Compliance Information: Batch #CS13RC: For further information contact Rosen Publishing, New York, New York at 1-800-237-9932.

Contents

Important Civilizations	4
What's a Dynasty?	6
Ancient Writings	8
China's Class System	12
Family Life	14
Important Beliefs	16
Ancient Chinese Inventions	20
Great Wall Facts	22
Glossary	23
Index	24

Important Civilizations

China is a country with a long, rich history. This Asian country is home to many mountains and rivers that have shaped the lives of people living there for thousands of years.

The Yangtze River and the Yellow River (also called the Huang He) are two of the most important rivers in Chinese history. Civilizations (sih-vuh-luh-ZAY-shunz) began to grow around these rivers thousands of years ago. A civilization is a society of people settled in one place that has developed writing, art, science, and government.

The civilizations that grew along the Yangtze and the Yellow Rivers in China were some of the oldest on Earth!

China

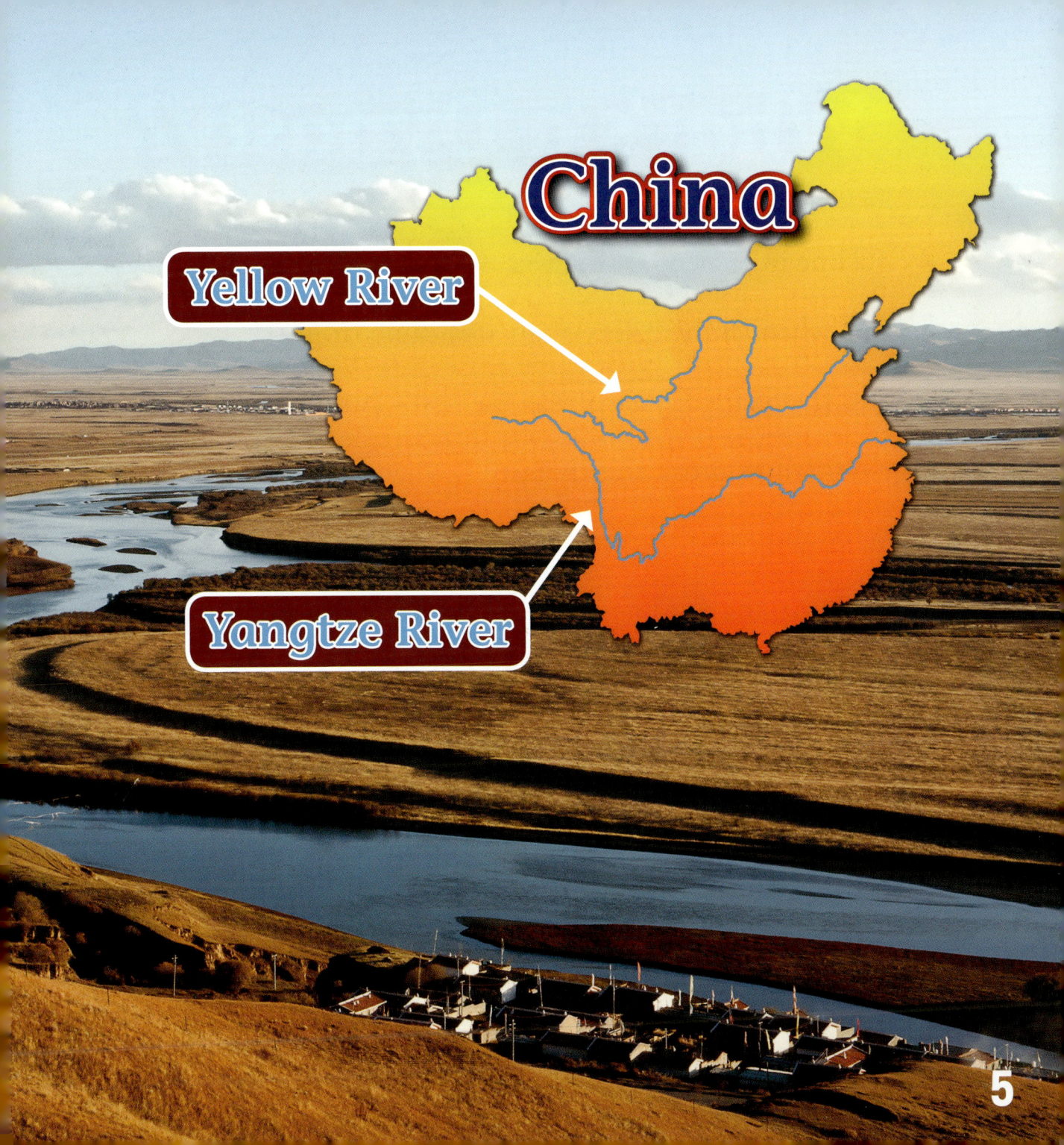

Yellow River

Yangtze River

5

What's a Dynasty?

Time in ancient China was measured in dynasties, or periods when all the rulers of an area came from the same family. The Shang Dynasty was the first Chinese dynasty to have written records. This dynasty is where recorded history in China begins.

Historians don't agree on when the Shang Dynasty began. The date for the beginning of this dynasty is believed to be between 1760 and 1520 BC. The date for the end is believed to be between 1122 and 1030 BC.

During the Shang Dynasty, people began using bronze, which is a common, yellow-brown metal that turns green over time.

7

Ancient Writings

We know about the Shang Dynasty because of the written records people kept during that time. But these weren't ordinary writings—some of them can be found on bones!

Ancient Chinese **priests** used to write on cow bones with special cracks to answer people's questions about the future. These are called oracle (OHR-uh-kuhl) bones. These writings can also be seen on tortoise shells. The oracle bones and shells give us a record of the leaders that ruled during this time and the history of the dynasty.

Some Chinese family names were carved onto oracle bones and can still be read today!

9

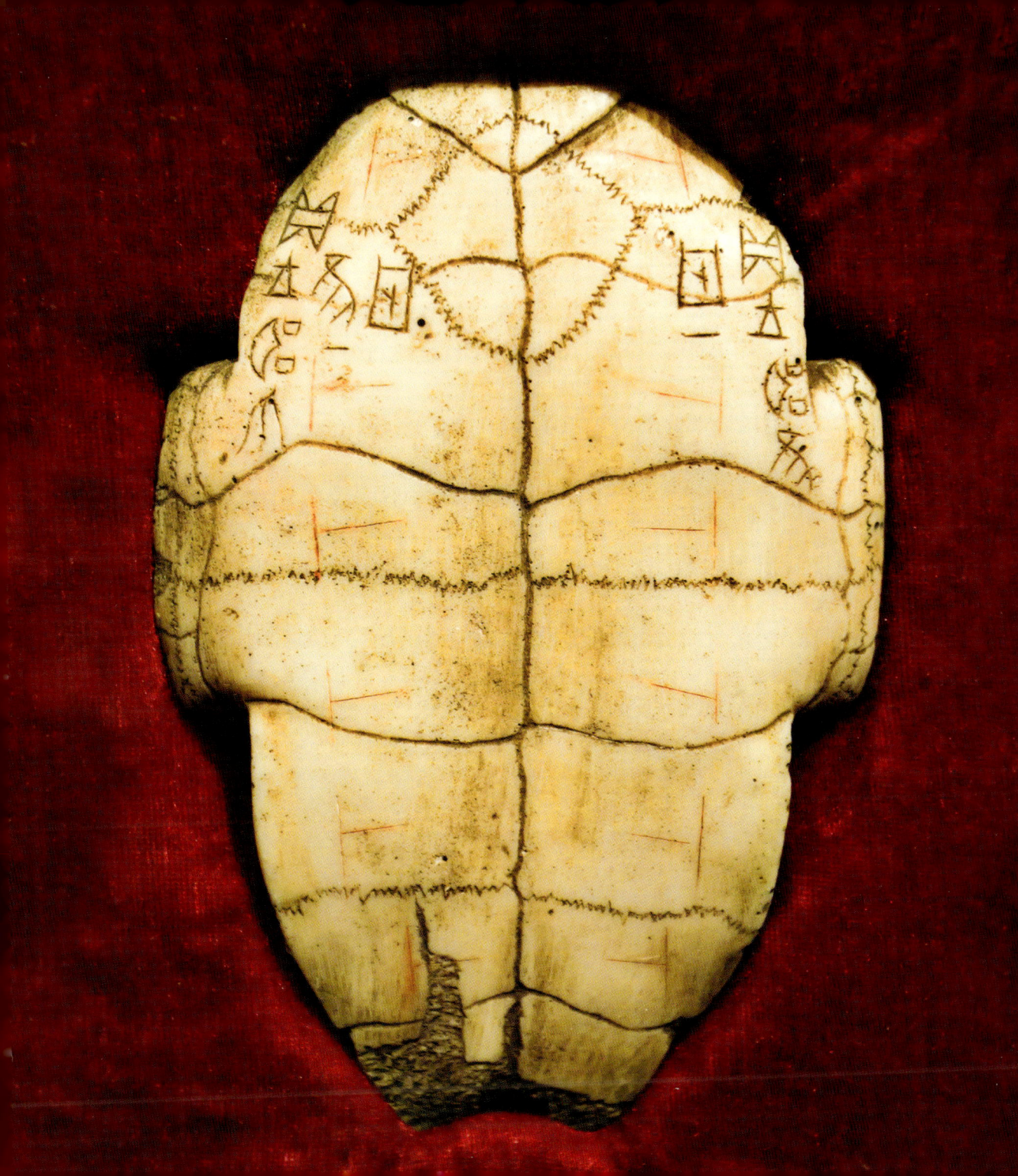

As time went on, Chinese people learned more advanced ways of writing. They began to use special characters to stand for words, much like the alphabet we use today.

In ancient China, writing was often seen as an art similar to painting. This artistic way of writing is called calligraphy (kuh-LIH-gruh-fee), which means "beautiful writing." It uses ink and a brush to create beautiful words on paper. Calligraphy used to be taught in ancient Chinese schools. It's still a popular art today in countries around the world!

Different kinds of calligraphy are created by holding the brush in different ways.

11

China's Class System

Calligraphy was one of many kinds of art made in ancient China. Artists were seen as talented, but they weren't valued members of society. There were **strict** social classes in ancient China. The upper class was made up of the richest and most important members of ancient Chinese society, such as the leader, or emperor. Government officials, **scholars**, and businesspeople were also part of the upper class.

The lower class was made up of soldiers, merchants, scientists, and the poor. They weren't very respected in ancient China.

The emperor was the leader of all China in ancient times. He was at the top of the upper class of Chinese society.

13

Family Life

Families in ancient China also had a strict **structure**. The father was the family leader. Women were ruled by their father until they married. Then, they were ruled by their husband. If their husband died, they were ruled by their oldest son. Ancient Chinese marriages were arranged by the parents, which meant the children had no say in the person they would marry.

Only boys went to school in ancient China. However, most boys helped their families on the farm or in the fields instead.

Today, both boys and girls go to school in China. That wasn't true in ancient times!

15

Important Beliefs

The family was the most important part of ancient Chinese life. People even believed that family members were still a part of their lives after they died. They would often ask their ancestors, or dead family members, to watch over them.

The people of ancient China held other important beliefs, too. They believed in many gods, but one had more power than others. He was known as "Heaven," and Heaven decided who the emperor would be.

Throughout Chinese history, many buildings have been made to honor Heaven. The Temple of Heaven is one such building that's still standing today!

17

One of the most important people during ancient times in China was Confucius (kuhn-FYOO-shus). He was a philosopher, or a thinker who taught others about how to live.

Confucius was born in 551 BC and first worked for the Chinese government. Later in his life, he became a teacher. He taught his students the importance of kindness and goodness. Confucius taught that everyone has duties towards others. He also taught about moderation, or the balance between too much and too little.

Confucius's students wrote down his teachings so they would live on after his death. People still practice his teachings and read about his life.

19

Ancient Chinese Inventions

Many important things were discovered and invented in ancient China. Gunpowder was first used during this time. It allowed the ancient Chinese to create fireworks thousands of years before we started using them on the Fourth of July! Paper was also used for the first time in ancient China.

Ancient China had many important roads. By 210 BC, there were over 4,000 miles (6,436 km) of roads in China! People began building the Great Wall of China during ancient times, too. They used the first wheelbarrows to help build the Great Wall!

Ancient China gave the world many other important things, too, such as kites and pasta!

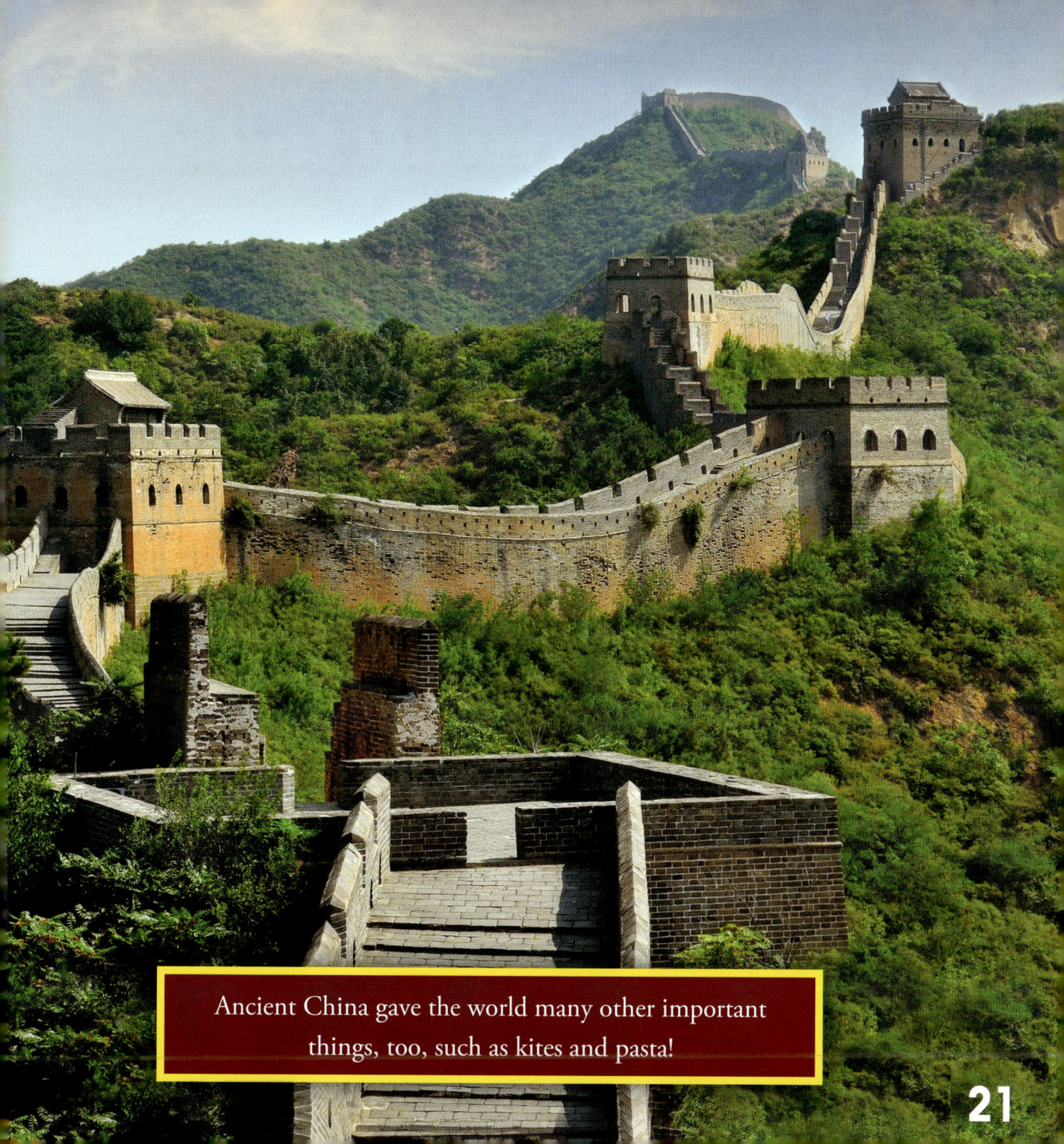

Great Wall Facts

- construction began over 2,000 years ago
- 5,500 miles (8,850 km) long 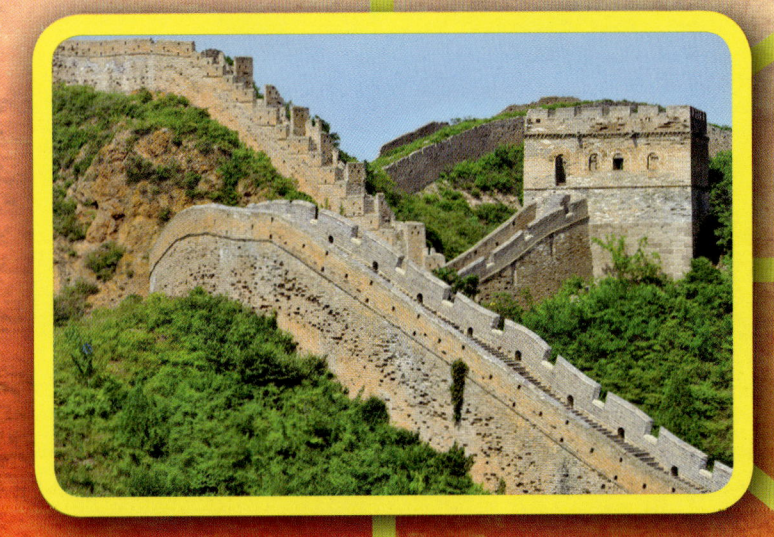
- 25 feet (7.6 m) tall
- 15 to 30 feet (4.6 to 9.1 m) wide at different points
- made from stone, soil, sticks, and bricks

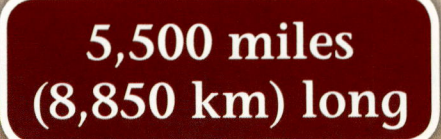

Glossary

historian (hih-STOHR-ee-uhn) A person who studies history.

priest (PREEST) A person who leads or performs religious activities.

scholar (SKAH-luhr) A person who has done advanced studying.

strict (STRIHKT) Absolute; kept with great care.

structure (STRUHK-chuhr) Something arranged in a clear pattern.

Index

art, 4, 10, 12

calligraphy, 10, 12

Confucius, 18

dynasty(ies), 6, 8

emperor, 12, 16

family(ies), 6, 8, 14, 16

gods, 16

Great Wall, 20, 22

gunpowder, 20

Heaven, 16

oracle bones, 8

paper, 10, 20

roads, 20

school, 14

social classes, 12

Temple of Heaven, 16

writing(s), 4, 6, 8, 10

Yangtze River, 4, 5

Yellow River, 4, 5